TALKING IT THROUGH

When Uncle Bob Died

Althea

Illustrated by Sarah Wimperis

Happy Cat Books

I found a butterfly on the window-sill.
Mum said it was dead.
I wanted to make it fly again. I took it outside and
threw it in the air, but it fell to the ground.

Leisure & Community Services

Please return this item by the last date stamped below, to the library from which it was borrowed.

Renewals
You may renew any item twice (for 3 weeks) by telephone or post, providing it is not required by another reader. *Please quote the number stated below.*

Overdue charges
Please see library notices for the current rate of charges for overdue items. Overdue charges are not made on junior books unless borrowed on adult tickets.

Postage
Both adult and junior borrowers must pay any postage on overdue notices.

19 OCT 2002	– 4 JUN 2005	
24 MAR 2003	17 MAR 2008	
	Renewals 0333 370 4700 arena.yourlondonlibrary.net/ web/bromley	

739.96

Mum said, 'When you are dead, you don't come alive again. That butterfly will always be dead. Let's go and bury it in the garden.'

'When you play wars and shoot each other dead, you know that it is only pretend. You can get up and run after the others again.'

'It's not like that when a person or animal is really dead. They will never get up again. It is very sad for us when it is someone we know.'

'All animals and people have to die one day.
Sometimes animals and people die because they have
a bad accident, or because they are very ill.'

'But usually, people don't die until they are very old,
and their bodies are tired and worn out.
When they die and their hearts stop beating,
they don't know anything about life any more.

We miss them, and it makes us very sad.'

Uncle Bob wasn't old when he died. It wasn't fair, I felt angry with him for dying. It made us all cry and feel very unhappy.

Mum said he had been very ill, and sometimes when a person is very ill, their body gets too tired to live any more.

Mum and Dad went to Uncle Bob's funeral, with Aunty Rose and my cousins, Sara and David. Dad said this was a time to think and talk and cry about Uncle Bob, and say goodbye to him. I wish I could have been there too.

His body was in a box, called a coffin, which was buried in the ground. Mum said she would take me to see where he is buried. She told me that some people want to have their bodies burnt when they die. This is called cremation.

I told my teacher about Uncle Bob and that he wasn't old. She asked if anyone in our class wanted to talk about friends or relations who had died.

Quite a lot of children had lost a gran or grandad. We talked about how sad we feel when someone dies. John said it gave him a pain in his chest.

Su said her cousin Robert had died in a car accident last holidays. She had been playing with him the day before. She went to his funeral, and his friends sang his favourite pop song.

Su said 'He was my age, I still can't really believe I won't see him again.'
She cried a bit when she told us.
Our teacher said it can help to talk about our feelings, and share our sadness.

Jamie said he had a baby brother, Tom, who died soon after he was born. Jamie went to see him in hospital. 'I gave him a picture I had painted for him. He was very tiny and he wiggled his toes.'

'When Mum came home she kept crying. She said she was too tired to play with me.
It's better now, we talk about my brother Tom, and Mum has a photograph of him by her bed.'

Sometimes when I wake up in the morning, I forget that Uncle Bob is dead, and I think he'll come and see us soon. Then I remember, and I feel all sad again.

I think about Su and Jamie and my other friends at school, and how sad it is for them too.

Aunty Rose and David and Sara often come to lunch
with us on Sundays. We want them to feel they are part
of one big family.

Sometimes, David and Sara want to talk about their dad and feel sad or happy about him and the things he did. At other times, we play silly games and we laugh a lot.

Sometimes, I think Sara pretends that her dad has gone away and will be back soon.

I expect it is hard for her to get used to it all at once.

When they have gone home again, we talk about what it was like when Uncle Bob used to come too. He had a very smily face and he always picked me up and gave me a big hug.

It is hard to believe that Uncle Bob is dead for ever and will never come back.

I have a photograph of him in my room. I shall always remember how he really used to listen when I talked to him.

One day Dad was ill. He stayed in bed all day and he didn't really want to play with me or talk much. I was very frightened. Perhaps he was going to die too, like Uncle Bob.

Mum found me crying in bed. She gave me a big hug.
'You silly old thing. He's only a bit ill. He will get better
very soon - just like you did when you had that nasty
cold last week.'

We are going on holiday soon with Aunty Rose and David and Sara. We will try to make it a happy holiday. Uncle Bob would have wanted us to enjoy it.

I'll always love and remember Uncle Bob. Mum says people live on through our memories.

HAPPY CAT BOOKS

Published by Happy Cat Books Ltd.
Bradfield, Essex CO11 2UT, UK

This edition published 2001
1 3 5 7 9 10 8 6 4 2

A CIP catalogue record for this book is available from the British Library

ISBN 1 903285 08 9 Paperback
ISBN 1 903285 09 7 Hardback

Printed in Hong Kong by Wing King Tong Co. Ltd.